2ND BN South Wales Borderers
24th Regiment.

D-DAY to VE-DAY.

The Naval & Military Press Ltd

Published by

The Naval & Military Press Ltd
Unit 5 Riverside, Brambleside
Bellbrook Industrial Estate
Uckfield, East Sussex
TN22 1QQ England

Tel: +44 (0)1825 749494

www.naval-military-press.com
www.nmarchive.com

In reprinting in facsimile from the original, any imperfections are inevitably reproduced and the quality may fall short of modern type and cartographic standards.

PREFACE

This booklet is divided into two parts; the first contains an outline of the activities of the 2/24th during the campaign in Europe from D day to VE day; the second, a somewhat detailed account of some of the more important actions in which the Battalion has fought.

It must be understood that it in no way sets out to be an official history but is intended rather to provide for those of us who were present, a momento for future years of the campaign through which we fought as members of the Battalion, and for those who were not present but who nevertheless take a live interest in the Battalion, a broad picture of our doings.

The writers, of whom there have been three and of whom Major J. T. Boon has made the largest contribution, have purposely avoided the mention of any person by name, as it was thought invidious to single out individuals when so many others have performed equally noteworthy acts which, however, for one reason or another, have passed unrecorded, and often, indeed, unnoticed.

HAMBURG
May 1945.

H. P. GILLESPIE

LIST OF AWARDS

DSO
    Lt-Col R. W. Craddock, MBE   Lt-Col F. F. S. Barlow

MC
    Capt A. F. Thompson   Major G. Dauncey
    Lt D. M. E. Randell   Major D. F. H. Collins
    Lt A. J. Booth   Capt G. R. Clarke (RAMC)
    Capt D. S. Stroud   Lt R. Kernick
    Lt D. H. Whittaker

DCM
    3907548 Sjt D. Edwards

MM
    3908898 Cpl L. Thomas   3910307 L/S W. J. Thomas
    3915955 L/S L. Thomas   3909937 Sjt A. Boocock
    4192066 Sjt G. F. Hulland   4075593 Sjt H. Phelps
    3907386 Cpl J. Lockhart   3911107 Pte D. R. Roberts
    3915927 Pte R. Jenkins   3909874 Pte S. G. Lloyd
    3915522 L/C H. C. Kenwood   3909600 Pte G. E. Carey
    4081319 Sjt D. Tough   3908764 CSM R. Cude
    14327980 Pte M. Murgatroyd   3910892 Pte G. Gallagher
    4080457 Cpl W. G. Cook   4074894 Pte S. G. Lewis
    3915930 Sjt M. Jones   14714719 Pte L. T. Allen

BEM
    3906425 Sjt W. B. Harrison

Croix-de-Guerre
    Major J. E. Thurn   3907152 L/S L. R. Smith
    14676236 Pte G. O'Sullivan

Mention-in-Despatches
    Lt E. V. Richards   Capt L. K. Pallister
    743923 Sjt P. L. Richards

C-in-C's Certificate
    Capt E. L. Thurn   Lt T. O'Reilly
    3907678 CSM T. H. Hughes   3907542 Cpl C. J. P. Dowd
    4074946 Cpl W. J. Powell   3056742 Sjt J. Milligan
    14676592 Pte J. Jacques   3907442 Sjt O. P. Cowan

PART I

January 1944 found the 2/24th forming part of 7 Inf Bde in 9 Armd Div. Unfortunately it had become obvious that the Division was losing priority and disquiet was felt that the Inf Bde might at best become a draft finding formation and at worst be disbanded. Accordingly, steps were taken to protect the interests of the 2/24th which as a regular battalion of a Regiment which has rendered such distinguished service to its country deserved a better fate. It so happened that two other regular battalions, the 2 ESSEX and the 2 GLOSTERS, were in the same plight and so 56 Bde came into being as an Independent Bde, composed of three regular bns. The badge of each Regiment contains the Sphinx as one of its symbols, and the sphinx was accordingly taken as the Bde sign, which it has retained ever since throughout all changes of formation and which obtained increasing respect as the campaign continued.

Because of the misfortune of 9 Armd Div, the Bn found itself at a disadvantage when compared to units which had been mobilized for a year or more. It was over 200 men below strength and up to D-7 was still receiving reinforcements. It was deficient of many articles of equipment. It had not during the Winter of 1943 enjoyed the training facilities and immunity from postings extended to mobilized formations. The bns of the Bde had not long worked together. The Battalion had, however, always preserved excellent discipline and a strong regimental pride to which can be attributed the fine record of achievement won in the ensuing campaign.

FRANCE

The invasion of NORMANDY was the greatest combined operation in history and anyone who took part in it realises how much its success was due to the careful planning which went before.

After a period of training in combined operations and several large scale invasion exercises, the Bn concentrated in a camp near SOUTHAMPTON. It was a tented camp in a dank wood, where the soil was always moist and the thick trees shut out even the brightest sun. Everyone lived in a state of feverish activity. Equipment was checked, ammunition scales studied, loading trials held, route marches done carrying the full, many assorted, complicated list of articles with which the assaulting soldier is loaded, reinforcements arrived and, in short, a thousand last minute preparations took place. It was a hectic, uncomfortable, anxious time and everyone looked forward to "D" Day.

About 10 days before "D" Day, briefing began. The camp was sealed and no-one was allowed outside without a special pass. The briefing was excellent and again one could not but be struck by the extreme care with which every thing had been planned. The Bde had known its role before. It was operating as a fourth Bde to 50(N) Div with the task of pushing through the initial bridgehead secured in the first assault by 231 Bde. No-one, however, knew where the landing was to take place nor any exact details. Briefing was therefore awaited with keen interest, and few who were present will forget sitting in a large tent on a boiling summer afternoon and learning that the Allies were landing in NORMANDY and that the Bn in particular was to land near ARROMANCHES and push swiftly inland to seize the high ground North of BAYEUX.

The careful preparations filled everyone with confidence. There was a lavish issue of all types of maps. There were Intelligence Summaries giving full details of enemy positions and identifications and even attempting to describe the bocage country which later presented such a tactical problem to commanders. From aerial photographs one could see every detail of the beaches and of the roads which led to the objective. Particularly useful were two magnificent models of the beach and the hinterland, accurate to the position of every hedgerow. It was reassuring to hear platoon commanders discussing where they would put their sections on D+1 and even more reassuring on D+1 to see them in those positions.

Finally, when all was ready, the Bn embarked at LYMINGTON on three USA LCsI and sailed to SOUTHAMPTON, where it stayed for two days. On the evening of 5 June it set sail for FRANCE and landed at 1200 hours 6 June on the coast of NORMANDY one mile East of ARROMANCHES.

The landing took place two hours later than was expected on none of the three appointed beaches, but otherwise all went according to plan. The coastal plain was flat and sandy and dominated by hills rising inland. After re-organising, the Bn at once pushed on. It dealt with a RADAR Station held by the enemy, and spent the night forming a close bridgehead round the important br at EAUX-SUR-AVRE, three miles from its objective.

Next morning the high ground North of BAYEUX was occupied. The companies dug in and patrolled into the outskirts of the town. The situation was extremely fluid. The attack on the coast and the deep British penetrations had thrown the enemy into confusion. Therefore, although we were in considerable strength at BAYEUX, the country behind was full of snipers and small bands of enemy trying to work their way back to the German lines. The papers with truth talked much of the low grade German coastal divisions composed of poor fighters, but in these divisions there were sub-units and individuals who fought with extreme bravery. Snipers especially had a hampering effect upon operations. They were very difficult to locate in such close country and British troops never knew whether they could with safety use any particular road or enter some field.

The Bn was on the extreme right of the British Army and it was part of its task to link up with the left of the American Forces along the line of the river AVRE. One joint post was to be formed at SULLY. When on D+1 "A" Company moved down to contact the Americans, they found the bridge and the Chateau to the West strongly held by the enemy. It was here on D+2 that the battle of SULLY was fought. Next day the First American Div was contacted.

The Bn remained North of BAYEUX until 10 June when the Bde came under command of 7 Armd Div with the task of following up the advance to VILLERS BOCAGE. Its first operation was to capture and hold five bridges over a stream running South from BAYEUX and forming the boundary with 231 Bde, who had now moved forward.

The country South of BAYEUX was very close. It was typical Bocage and consisted of an irregular pattern of rectangular fields and orchards. The fields were bounded by earth banks from 4 to 5 feet high and in the banks trees grew. Good observation was impossible, being limited to the breadth of the fields. Even the hills failed to give OPs. Woods and copses abounded. It was difficult country in which to attack, because observed fire could not be brought down on enemy positions. Shooting was done off the map. Attacking troops only found out where the enemy was, when they bumped him and the tanks often only spotted anti-tank guns when it was too late. Control was particulary difficult.

The next 7 weeks saw the hardest fighting which the Bn experienced. It was a crucial time. As yet there were few troops ashore, the bridgehead was small and at all costs the enemy had to be prevented from re-grouping his forces and making an organised attack upon our positions. The only way to keep the initiative was to attack ourselves. There followed the long series of containing attacks made along the TILLY-CAUMONT road, at TILLY, VERRIERES, LINGEVRES, HOTTOT, LE LION VERT and ST GERMAIN D'ESTOT; all fierce, bloody battles.

After handing over the bridges to the 2 DEVONS the Bn reverted back to 50(N) Div and took up a defensive position at BUCEELS, a small village on a cross roads North of TILLY. BUCEELS was a cursed spot, regularly stonked by enemy mortars and artillery. The Bn learnt there three lessons. First, the importance of patrolling. Some excellent patrols were made to TILLY, bringing back vital information. Second, the importance of really deep digging, heavily emphasized when Bn HQ was shelled and mortared for two hours and the MO killed and the Padre wounded. Third, the importance of siting HQs sufficiently far back for them to carry out their routine work without unnecessary danger.

From BUCEELS the Bn moved to ELLON, which was a rest area, though the two AGRAs which surrounded the village made it anything but restful. Here an operation was planned with 148 RAC but did not take place.

The next move was to LA SENAUDIERE on 23 June where the Bn passed under command of 69 Bde of 50(N) Div. LA SENAUDIERE was typical of many position which the Bn held. The country was extremely close and since the enemy's movements could not be seen, continuous patrolling was necessary to discover his intentions. Moreover, our positions were regularly mortared and life is a strain for all when any moment brings down a crump of shells and when the trees make every shell an airburst.

The Bn's next position was LA BUTTE North of a little village called GRANVILLE on the maps, but COURVILLE by the inhabitants. Behind the village lay the thick, sombre mass of the Bois De St Germain. Between the BOIS and the village of ST GERMAIN D'ECTOT ran the TILLY—CAUMONT road. It took a month of hard fighting and patrolling before the Bn had battled its way from LA BUTTE to ST GERMAIN D'ECTOT. The attack on GRANVILLE and the La Chapelle cross roads was the Bn's most costly operation.

The month spent at LA BUTTE and GRANVILLE saw the turning point in the battle of NORMANDY. When the position was first occupied there was tension in the air. Every movement brought down mortar fire. At first patrolling was intensive on both sides. The Germans would creep up to our lines in small parties, firing tracer from their spandaus hoping to draw fire, but soon the Bn gained the ascendancy. It is impossible to praise too highly those who carried out these patrols in close, difficult country, in all weathers, by day and by night. Tribute was paid to the effectiveness of their efforts by an officer cadet captured by a "C" Company patrol. He came from 2 Panzer Div, acknowledged by the Germans to be their best division. 2 Panzer Div was opposite the Bn and he said that our patrolling was so intensive that the division had formed a special anti-patrol platoon of one Lieutenant and 50 volunteers to counteract its effect. He was made prisoner his first time out.

As the operations around GRANVILLE developed, the Bn underwent a severe testing. After the first attack, two companies were left holding an exposed forward position not 50 yards from the enemy, overlooked and registered by enemy mortars. It was very exhausting to stay there for more than a few days at a time, but the position was held, and finally when the Bn attacked again, the enemy were driven back in complete confusion. It was at this time that the German front broke, and almost overnight one began to think of advancing in terms of miles instead of yards.

All of the Bn who fought at GRANVILLE pay tribute to the artillery. Throughout the fighting the artillery was magnificent. The enemy was unable to move by day and, fresh enemy companies which entered the line at full strength, would at the end of a week be reduced to 25%. It was fortunate that two particularly fine Regiments the 86 Field (Hertfordshire Yeomanry) and the 90 Field (City of London), were in support of the Bn. Co-operation between the artillery and the Company Commanders has never been better. Several conducted shoots acting themselves as FOOs. It was, however, the counter-battery and the counter-mortar activities of the Regiments which were especially appreciated. If one enemy gun fired on the Bn, a regiment replied, if a troop or battery an AGRA answered.

On 1 August "D" Company captured ST GERMAIN D'ECTOT after a model company attack in co-operation with AVREs, Flails and Crocodiles. The Bn at once pushed forward to the LAUNAY ridge. There was a feeling of achievement in the air. The LAUNAY ridge had been prepared by the enemy as a defensive position, but he abandoned it without a fight. The hillside was honeycombed with slit trenches and dugouts. Enemy equipment littered the fields and lanes. A few dead lay in the forward positions. Everywhere, there was evidence of dis-organised flight. From a German OP on the ridge, the British tanks could be seen fighting miles ahead on mount PINCON. The long stretch of country between was free from enemy. It was the beginning of the German break-up.

After the capture of the LAUNAY ridge the Bde was given four days rest at CHOUAIN, not far from BUCEELS, now very much quieter than it was in June. The Bde left 50(N) Div and 30 Corps and passed into 59 Div in 12 Corps. This Division had just forced the crossing of the ORNE and the Bn moved across NORMANDY in time to take part in the extension of the bridgehead.

At the point where it was crossed, the ORNE runs through a steep gorge. The bridgehead had seen some very fierce fighting and was a disagreeable piece of country full of smashed equipment, dead, broken houses, flies, wasps and mosquietoes. It smelt strongly of Germans with that sickly, sweet smell which hangs about their positions.

On 10 August the Bn moved southwards in the bridgehead and by night took up a very precarious position at COURT GENETS not far from THURY HARCOURT. There were two high features across a steep valley and these were each occupied by two companies. Bn HQ and the remainder of the Bn remained across the valley. In taking up position, the companies fought sharp actions with German rearguards. When day broke, for the two subsequent days, they were subjected to heavy fire from enemy artillery, mortars and Nebelwerfers (Moaning Minnies). Casualties were heavy. The only means of communication with the companies were two roads which were overlooked by day and registered by night. As usual the Bn ambulance jeep drivers did magnificent work in bringing back the wounded under fire.

The shelling slowly lessened and the Bn resumed the advance, moving on 14 August behind a forward body to occupy a hill near ESSON South of THURY HARCOURT. The enemy allowed the Bn to reach the hill and when they were on top shelled it heavily. However, that night, another move forward was made in what was by now a standard fashion. Strong fighting patrols pushed forward to the next feature, occupied it and signalled the rest of the Bn to follow.

The next move on 17 August was to the Northern edge of the FALAISE pocket about 6 miles SW of FAILAISE where the Bde took over from a Bde of 53 DIV. The FALAISE pocket was an extraordinary sight. Bn was dug in on high ground and at night across the pocket one could see the flash of American guns firing towards us from the other side. In between lay the trapped German forces. All night tremendous artillery concentrations thrashed down upon them and the area was ringed with fire. By day wave upon wave of aircraft came over to destroy their transport. However, disorganised and trapped though they were, they were still capable of stiff resistance as the fight at LEVAL wood on 20 August proved.

After leaving LEVAL, the Bde changed its fmn once more and became part of 49 DIV, who were pressing forward to the SEINE. The Bn followed behind and did not come into action again until it forced the crossing of the River RISLE at PONT AUDEMER on 26 August. This again was a most difficult operation, carried out by night with very little time for reconnaissance. Two companies crossed and when dawn broke they were established on the steep cliffs which rise to the EAST of the town. Communication with them was impossible except by line, because the part of the town, between them and the rest of the Bn, was still held by the enemy. It was a fine feat of arms to cross by night and move through the enemy's positions.

From PONT AUDEMER the Bde moved to clear up the FORET DE BRETONNE, a large forest in one of the loops of the SEINE. Previous experience with woods and forests had not been happy. The BOIS DE ST GERMAIN in particular was a bogey filled with mines and German positions. The Bn was in reserve for the first stage of the operation. Unfortunately, while in reserve it was ordered to mop up a small pocket of enemy who were troubling the gunners. "D" Company went to attack, but while forming up encountered heavy mortar fire and suffered 18 casualties, including several full ranks. This was an example of how small actions frequently proved more costly than full scale attacks. Next day, towards evening the Bn was given the task of driving straight through the centre of the wood to MAILLERAYE, a village on the left bank of the SEINE. The order was received with gloom because not many hours of daylight remained and because the Intelligence was mistrusted. From bitter experience it had been learnt that disorganised enemy, who at Corps or Divisional level seemed tired of war and eager to give themselves up as prisoners, behaved quite differently on the ground, however, the forebodings were unnecessary and the manoeuvre was carried out without loss. It proved to be one of these brilliant strokes by which our G-O-C builds up such confidence. The approach to the SEINE was interesting. The roads were lined with dead horses, guns and smashed vehicles. As the Bn raced through the forest, hundreds of the burnt out trucks could be seen amongst the trees. The destruction on the roads was nothing to the chaos rounds the ferry sights. There every type of equipment lay in confusion, trucks, waggons, cookers, anti-tank guns, AA guns, 8.8 mm, gun carriages and tanks all in disorder. In the Bn area alone over 300 vehicles were counted. The fields were full of horses, hundreds and hundreds of them from chargers to shires, left behind by the retreating forces. Prisoners poured in; over 400 in 24 hrs. Apart from the destruction, as our leading troops came out of the trees, it was moving to see the people coming streaming from their farms, across the green fields to shake their hands and say, "Maintenant nous sommes contacts".

A few days later the Bn crossed the SEINE and took part in the capture of LE HAVRE. Full details of this operation can be found elsewhere. It is sufficient to say that the Twenty Fourth did outstandingly well, and that it was largely due to the initial assault by 56 Bde upon the outer German defences that the whole operation was so successful. It was no ordinary feat to capture a great city and take eleven thousand prisoners in a two day attack.

After the capture of LE HAVRE the battalion had a four days rest at LILLEBONNE which was rendered very pleasant by a quantity of champagne, cognac and butter taken from the German food dumps in LE HAVRE.

As a tail piece to the campaign in France, here are two tales which pleased everyone. A CMP on the bridge over a canal was heard saying to the fury of other Regiments, "I bet anyone that once the South Wales Borderers come we will be advancing again in three days", while a gunner greeted our leading company with "We've been waiting for you!". Small things, but they show that the 2/24th had not been unworthy of its past.

BELGIUM AND HOLLAND

When the spoils of Le Havre had been consumed, the battalion set off on its journey across the Pas-de-Calais into Belgium, and after two days concentrated in the village of ITAGHEM, which lies about 10 miles due south of the ANTWERP—TURNHOUT canal.

At this time the battalion was in the 1st Corps, which was operating under command of 1st Canadian Army. The object of the Army was to clear all of Holland south of the River WAAL, which included the Island of WALCHEREN and the HOOK of HOLLAND. 2nd Canadian Corps were given everything to the west of ANTWERP and 1st Corps everything to the east. Thus it was that the first obstacle which 49th Division had to cross was the ANTWERP—TURNHOUT canal, a deep waterway about 40 ft wide and easily defended.

On the 25 September, the battalion moved from ITAGHEM and that night, under cover of darkness, crossed the ANTWERP—TURNHOUT canal and dug in on the western side of a small and heavily shelled bridgehead which had been established by the 1/4th K.O.Y.L.I. At 0230 hours on the 26th the enemy attacked in strength along the canal bank from the west in an effort to capture the bridge and eliminate all troops in the bridgehead. "D" Coy, who had just finished digging in put up a stout fight, but the enemy pressed on, shouting out in perfect English "Stop firing, you bloody fools", and other catch phrases. Two platoons of "D" Coy were virtually overrun and the remainder of the Company rallied round Bn HQ. "C" Coy of the Leicesters, who were in a counter-attack role, were on the spot very quickly and by 0700 hours had restored the situation. Meanwhile, the enemy had been counter-attacking "B" Coy's position continuously since 0230 hours, and as it was a very dark night it was impossible to shoot to kill until the Germans were within 60 yards of our positions.

Throughout all these attacks, "B" Coy remained firm and by firing all their small arms weapons with the greatest accuracy, succeeded in inflicting very heavy casualties on the enemy. One platoon showed great bravery, particularly amongst the NCOs, in shooting at very close range and maintaining a high and accurate rate of fire against an enemy who was by far numerically superior. This platoon earned an M.C. and two M.Ms for this action, an account of which appeared in the Daily Telegraph. Afterwards, behind a hedge only 40 yards in front of their positions, no less than 43 dead Germans were counted. At 0930 hours the Bosche launched his third and last counter-attack, this time against "A" Coy. With the aid of a troop of tanks, "A" Coy were able to make a bag of 40 prisoners and 16 killed with very little loss to themselves. During the day, the whole bridgehead had been very heavily shelled and Bn HQ had three direct hits. It was due to the battalion remaining firm against these hard and fierce counter-attacks that the bridgehead was maintained and the crossing of the canal assured. The next day "B" Coy reported that the enemy were digging in just in front of them, and so, with a troop of tanks, they attacked, forcing the enemy to withdraw and enabling the Commanding Officer to push forward the whole battalion to the village of RYJKEVORSEL, thereby extending the perimeter of the bridgehead.

For the next few days the bridgehead was not extended owing to a change of plan and the battalion remained in the area, being shelled every day and sending out patrols each night. The reason for this delay was because it had been decided to switch the main effort of the Division in a drive from TURNHOUT to TILBURG. To cover this movement and to obtain surprise, the battalion was ordered to make an attack due north of RYJKEVORSEL mainly as a feint, although we were not told this at the time. Accordingly on the 4th October, "A" and "B" Coys formed up together with a troop of tanks to attack two known enemy localities which had been responsible for a lot of mortaring and shelling. Zero hour was set for 1515 hours, and both companies started on time. Unfortunately, the ground which had to be crossed was very open, and as soon as the advance started, both companies came under very heavy small arms and Spandau fire from the left flank, which caused a considerable number of casualties. The troop of tanks moved forward to try and deal with this, but owing to the soft nature of the ground, the two leading tanks became bogged. The other two eventually found another way round and started to shoot up everything in the area of a lime kiln and brickworks, which was the centre of the enemy locality. By calling down artillery on this target, and under cover of the supporting fire from these tanks, the two companies were able to move forward, but by this time it was getting dark. Before reaching the final objective, which would have entailed a further flanking movement by "B" Company, the Commanding Officer ordered "A" and "B" Companies to dig in for the night. The Brigadier decided that the feint had achieved its purpose, and during the night the battalion was ordered to withdraw to their normal positions. During the night and early next morning some great work was done by the Brigade REME in pulling out five anti-tank guns and two carriers which had been bogged within 250 yards of the enemy.

On the morning of the 5 October, the battalion started to move Eastwards and join in the main effort towards TILBURG. However, we had first to take over a position which was held by the Recce as they were urgently needed on the main Divisional front. The area which we took over was very spread out and consisted of forest and undergrowth, so that platoons were in many cases on their own, forming standing patrols. While we were in this position there was little enemy activity, until at 2150 hours the battalion had an extremely heavy artillery concentration on the centre of the area.

On the 8 October, the battalion handed over to BROCKFORCE, which consisted of the LAA Regt and some A/Tks acting as infantry. We moved at 1400 hours through TURNHOUT and up the TILBURG road to join the Divisional advance on TILBURG, and went into a reserve position in the village of POPPEL which lies on the DUTCH-BELGIAN border. The enemy was quite active in this area and the Lincolns, whom we relieved, had had a pretty tough time of it. The Germans had been counter-attacking with TIGER tanks, supported by quite a lot of guns. This we soon realised because the village of POPPEL came in for a lot of shelling during the time we were there. Two attempts were made by the Division to push on towards TILBURG, but the ground afforded a wonderful defensive position for the enemy, and they laid mines extensively. It was therefore decided that 30 Corps would take TILBURG from the east with the 51st Highland Division whilst we contained as many Germans as possible on our side of TILBURG. Accordingly the battalion remained on the POPPEL front until the 17 October, during which time it patrolled extensively and, with the help of a lot of harassing fire, made as much nuisance of itself as possible. The result of all this was that when TILBURG was eventually taken a considerable number of Germans were cut off between TILBURG and POPPEL.

As a result of the decision that 30 Corps would deal with TILBURG and St HERTOGENBOSCH, 1st Corps moved over to the 2nd Canadian Corps sector in preparation for an advance towards ROSENDAAL and the LOWER RHINE. Accordingly, the battalion moved to the village of BRECHT on the 18 October and took over from a squadron of Canadian Armoured Recce. The Brigade attack north to capture LOENHOUT was timed for the 20th of October, and during the two days before this attack there was considerable shelling by both sides as well as active patrolling. The battalion's part in this attack was to attack and capture the village of BEEKHOVEN and then act as reserve battalion for the advance to LOENHOUT. By taking the village of BEEKHOVEN it meant that the main road from BRECHT to WUSTWEZEL was clear for half its length and 146 Brigade would be able to advance on WUSTWEZEL without being held up at the start.

At 1000 hours on the 20 October, the battalion, supported by a squadron of tanks attacked down the main road to BEEKHOVEN. "D" Coy were used as fire company, and "A" and "B" companies attacked on either side of the road under a good artillery barrage. Opposition was heavy, particularly from small arms fire and some mortar detachments. The Germans were fighting as individualists, and a Spandau which had lain hidden while the tanks passed would suddenly open up on the infantry from the rear. The whole attack developed into little section battles, and it was not until 1215 hours that every sniper and post had been accounted for. Even then, when the objective had been reached, there was a lot of individual sniping and Spandau fire. Two German officers and 92 ORs were taken prisoner during this attack, and our casualties amounted to 2 Officers and 3 ORs killed and 22 ORs wounded. The success of this attack enabled 146 Brigade to get cracking sooner than had been expected. The next day the battalion moved up to a reserve position just south of LOENHOUT. The recce party, which had gone on ahead to STONEBRIDGE, got involved in a counter-attack with 5 TIGERS on the 1st Leicesters, and after an awkward moment and a severe artillery concentration coming through LOENHOUT, succeeded in getting back to the battalion intact.

The next day, the Division was relieved by the 104 American Infantry Division (The Timber Wolves). This Division had not seen active service before and were most interested in the way we did things. Although they were very green at the time they were to prove themselves a fine Division later on in the campaign.

On the 24th, the battalion moved to take over from the Canadians in the village ESSCHEN on the DUTCH-frontier. This was a very warm take over, as the Bosche had 30 SP Guns as well as a lot of field guns. He must also have had a large quantity of ammunition which he was determined to shoot off before eventually withdrawing behind the RHINE. All day the Recce Party was shelled and when the battalion arrived they received a very warm welcome. One unlucky shell landed in the middle of two stretcher jeeps, killing the doctor and MT Sergeant, and wounding the Medical Sgt and nine others, all of whom were specialist personnel. The shelling continued during the night and all the following day whilst the next operation was being planned.

The Divisional objective was to capture the town of ROSENDAAL and exploit to the banks of the river WAAL or LOWER RHINE. Accordingly, at 0100 hours on the 26th, "D" Coy crossed the start line in a silent attack to make a hole in the enemy defences by capturing a wood which we had patrolled and knew was occupied by the enemy. All would have gone well if it had not been for the artificial moonlight which was being used on the Corps front. "D" Coy, moving forward under cover of a very dark night were suddenly silhouetted to the great satisfaction of about half a dozen Spandau positions. Thus the whole surprise of the silent attack was ruined. It was not until 0500 hours that the position was clarified and the light switched off. "D" Coy then moved round under cover of darkness and attacked from a different flank. They reached their objective at 0700 hours and the Essex were passed through with two squadrons of tanks to continue the advance.

Next day, the Divisional attack was well under way and the battalion found itself being moved about the battle area, giving right flank protection and looking after some enemy who were being a nuisance in the NISPEN area. Before the infantry attack on ROSENDAAL was launched, the 60th Heavy AA Regt fired concentrated airbursts over the town for an hour and a half, which so unnerved the population and defenders that as soon as it stopped, they withdrew, and the Recce and tanks were able to drive straight into the city. While sitting outside ROSENDAAL, the battalion had come into contact with the most extensive minefields they had met since the GRANVILLE days in July. The Assault Pioneer Pl did great work in clearing these, many of which were "R" mines.

On the 3 November the advance continued beyond ROSENDAAL with the object of clearing the South bank of the WAAL and finally capturing the town of WILHELMSTADT. The country here was particulary difficult as the enemy had flooded the dykes and the fields were about 4 feet under water, only the roads themselves remained above the floods and they were covered by spandau posts on fixed lines. As a consequence all operations had to be carried out during darkness with everyone dug in along the roads by first light. There was never room to deploy more than one platoon at a time and so the battle developed into a series of platoon attacks with platoons leapfrogging their way down the roads and securing cross-roads and road junctions.

On the 3 November the battalion crossed the river MARK passing "A" and "B" Coys over first by a kapok footbridge to enlarge the right flank of 146 Bde bridgehead. They were followed by "D" Coy. Like all bridgeheads this one came in for some considerable shelling. On the following day 146 Bde took over the entire responsibility for the bridgehead allowing the battalion to withdraw to OUDCASTEL.

The battalion was then given the task of crossing the river further West and on the 5 November "D" Coy were to cross over and capture a small village on the far side and enable "A" and "B" Coys to pass through them. During "D" Coy's move forward they encountered a company of the GLOSTERS who were fighting a battle on the road immediately in front of them. This involved a considerable delay and it was not until 0800 hours that "D" Coy were in a position to carry out their assault on the final objective. About this time a message was received saying that the LINCOLNS were already in the village and ordering "D" Coy to move forward forthwith and take over from them. "D" Coy therefore moved down the road towards the village. Unfortunately the message was quite incorrect, for when the leading troops got within 100 yards the enemy opened fire with about 4 or 5 well concealed spandaus. The road was open with water on both sides. The leading platoon could find no cover. Casualties were heavy and the company were pinned down. An artillery smoke screen was put down and under the cover of this two platoons were able to extricate themselves. It was not however until dark that the third platoon was able to get back. This platoon spent a very uncomfortable day within 100 yards of the enemy but gave a good account of itself and performed a number of feats of gallantry in bringing in wounded.

On the withdrawal of "D" Coy a heavy artillery barrage was put down and "B" Coy following it closely, succeeded in taking the objective. As soon as "B" Coy were in position, "A" Coy was pushed through and around to the West of the town of WILHELMSTADT which was being assaulted by the LINCOLNS. From here "A" Coy made a diversion to enable the LINCOLNS to make the final assault which went in and secured the town.

The capture of WILHELMSTADT marked the end of all resistance South of the WAAL and the battalion was able to return to OUDCASTEL for a few days rest.

On the 15 November, we moved from the Canadian Army into the Second Army which was pushing forward towards VENLO, a town on the River MAAS. The battalion concentrated in the small town of LILLE-ST-HUBERT which gave a foretaste of what the conditions on this front were like. The area was strewn with mines of all types and sizes; the going was very soft; the roads few and bad and the pace of any advance perforcedly slow.

On the 22 November the battalion started to move forward in the assault towards VENLO, pushing through heavily wooded country with only cart-tracks, along which it was impossible to move wheeled vehicles. "A" and "B" Coys initially led the battalion attack. Opposition from the enemy was little, but shelling and heavy mining made the advance slow and laborious. "D" Coy were passed through on to the final objective where they were very heavily stonked by the guns of the Siegfried line firing across the river. The weather was atrocious, the whole countryside being turned into a sea of mud. The anti-tank guns were bogged down for three hours. The only vehicles which could be used for maintenance were "kangaroos" which proved themselves quite invaluable for bringing forward food, ammunition and greatcoats. The following day the advance churned its way forward under similar conditions of mines, shells, rain and mud.

Road conditions were now so bad, it was decided to switch the axis of the attack and capture BLERYCK a suburb of VENLO on the West bank of the MAAS, from a north-westerly direction. However before plans for this could crystalise the Division was relieved by 15(S) Division and placed once more under command of the Canadian Army. As a result the battalion moved on the 30 November up to NIJMEGEN and thence into the salient on the North bank of the WAAL, where it was to remain throughout the winter.

HOLLAND.

On 1 December the Bn moved on to the "Island". The "island", with which we were to become very familiar, is that area of land held between the two branches of the Rhine — Neder Rhine and the Waal, which figured so prominently in the fighting of the Airborne Troops attempting to seize Arnhem earlier in the year. It is joined to the mainland at Nijmegen by two bridges — a road bridge consisting of one enormous metal span and a railway bridge of three spans, the centre one of which the enemy had successfully demolished. The "island" itself is a rich agricultural area chequered by orchards but otherwise open and flat, each field separated from the next by a sizeable dyke.

Our first position was round ELST, a small town on the main road to ARNHEM, where the traces of previous battles still remained in the form of both German and British derelict tanks. We were in fairly close contact with the enemy but were more worried by the knowledge that most of the island was below river level and was only saved from flooding by a high bund which encircled it and which could at anytime be blown up by the enemy. We had in fact only been there 3 days when one evening at dusk a shattering explosion was heard. Reports came in a few hours later that the water was rising in all the dykes at an alarming rate followed shortly afterwards by a report from our forward Coy — "A" Coy, that the canal on their front had broken its bank and that water was pouring across the fields. It became evident that the enemy had blown the "bund" and the "island" was threatened with becoming submerged. "A" Coy had to be withdrawn slightly at midnight — an operation which involved at least one section swimming out of their post and a considerable loss of kit. During the night other adjustments of positions had to be made but by dawn the Bn was established astride roads which were fortunately built on embankments and therefore dry, and beyond everyone being extremely wet and somewhat bewildered, was able to face the barren stretch of water surrounding it without undue alarm. "A" Coy's evacuation was not made any easier by the fact that the enemy chose the same moment to launch an attack, but this Coy dealt out such effective punishment that they were able to wade out unmolested. The next days followed uneventfully, the water gradually rising, necessitating numerous readjustments of position but never making our area wholly untenable. It was a life of rubber boots and damp socks, boats and "weasels" — a type of amphibious tracked vehicle.

After ELST we had a few days rest in Nijmegen, then back again for another fortnight to the "island". In the middle of December we moved over to the western sector — ZETTEN, where we spent a reasonably enjoyable Christmas and had numerous successful clashes with the enemy. An account of our doings in this sector are included in Part II. The water had now receded a trifle although in many areas it was still 6 ft deep and necessitated moving about in "ducks" and "weasles". The Bn, however, had an admirable opportunity of learning a little watermanship.

Towards Christmas it began to freeze and the water rapidly became covered with ice. This of course made patrolling difficult as a few steps would cause so much noise that any movement could be heard at night over great distances.

After a short spell in a reserve area at RESSEN the Bn went back to Nijmegen for a rest of 5 days. But this was rudely curtailed and the Bn was ordered to move at once to the ANDELST sector on 19 January. It appeared that as we had suspected when we were previously in this sector, the enemy had determined to capture ZETTEN and with it the outpost line which was in the centre of the village and somewhat isolated from the rest of the Bn.

They had attacked ZETTEN on 16 January and after bitter fighting had infiltrated behind the outposts: it was estimated that the enemy force was about a Bn in strength. 56 Bde were therefore concentrated with the object of recapturing ZETTEN. The Glosters were committed on 18 January to strenghten up the Bn holding the sector, and the ESSEX and ourselves were ordered to attack on 20 January and recapture the town. We were on the left and organised the attack in 4 phases. In support we had two tps of 6 Cdn Armd Regt, who, however, found the icy road conditions made their movement very hazardous. The first two phases were completed according to plan although the house clearing made progress slow. The third phase, however, entailed capturing the "Castle" at HEMMEN, which, from our previous experiences, made us expect that it would be a difficult operation. During the afternoon "A" Coy which was carrying out this phase moved forward and soon encountered heavy fire from the "castle" and the surrounding outbuildings. By dark they had succeeded in establishing themselves in some neighbouring houses but could make no further progress. It was decided therefore that "D" Coy should take on the "castle" at first light on 21 January. Although one of "A" Coy's forward Pls was counterattacked early on 21st, "D" Coy's attack went forward as planned, and in spite of considerable opposition the "castle" was captured by teatime. To everyones' surprise no less than 120 enemy then emerged from the ruins and surrendered to the bewildered but proud platoon which carried out the final assault. During the two days fighting the Bn took some 208 prisoners and our own casualties were only 6 killed and some 40 wounded.

The following day was spent in clearing the area and towards evening the Bde having completed its task of recapturing ZETTEN and knocking out a complete enemy Bn into the bargain, was relieved and withdrawn into rest deservedly pleased with itself. This battle was fought in blinding snow and bitter cold: the Bn had two cases of frostbite.

About 26 January we moved back onto the island into the BEMMEL sector. The ground was still covered with snow and ice and all patrolling had to be done in snow-suits. The frost went on 6 February and the 2nd Army offensive to clear the area between the Maas and Rhine started on 8 February. Our initial part in this battle was to create a diversion with fire and our contribution therefore was limited to 1500 rounds from our 3" Mortar Platoon. We were near enough to be duly impressed by the air and artillery preliminary bombardment. From Bemmel we moved into the HALDEREN sector which bore an unsavory reputation owing to its close contact with the enemy (in places not more than 50 yds). However our experience there in no way supported this reputation and beyond the odd stonk and two casualties from enemy mines our stay was not eventful.

At the end of February the Bn moved into Nijmegen for 14 days rest: the first rest period which we had had for many weeks. "Rest" is perhaps a misnomer, as the period was marked by a succession of church parades, CO's parades, dances and Offrs' parties all of which sufficed to fill in ones time very successfully. We were lucky in that the 2nd Bn Band visited us at this period and was able to play at several concerts. One other incident during this rest is worthy of mention — on 1 March we were warned to relieve 53 Div in the Reichswald battle. The following day we sent recce parties down to GOCH and, although the plan was cancelled later that day, it gave some of the

Bn the satisfaction of crossing on to German soil and of seeing some of the complete devastation wrought by our air and artillery bombardment of German towns and villages: hardly a house or farm was left untouched, whole villages were reduced to piles of rubble. The Siegfried Line was impressive only for its rather desolate and devastated remains, white flags still fluttered from the tops of each farm but of civilian life there was nothing to be seen. For many of us it was an aweinspiring but wholly satisfactory spectacle.

On 11 March the Bn returned to the ZETTEN sector on the Island, where it had been before in December and again in January for the Bde counter attack. We found it very changed from our previous stay; the ice and floods had all vanished and ZETTEN itself bore some very rude scars from the January battle. One company was allotted an area round the castle, in the grounds of which there still remained a satisfactory number of Bosche corpses. This period was notable for the numerous near misses scored by flying bombs in the Bn area and the very good patrols carried out, some of which penetrated to the banks of the Upper Rhine. The Bn also executed a company night raid on the village of Randwijk. This was done by A Company, and involved the difficult task of clearing a large number of houses by night. The operation was carefully planned and went without a hitch. It had been hoped that the operation would provide a chance of bagging some Bosche, but those which were found, barricaded themselves into the village church and against its solid walls our infantry weapons proved of no avail. By the time the withdrawal was due to begin the enemy although severely knocked about, could not be extricated from their stronghold and the Company had to leave them behind. It was subsequently learnt that this operation was all part of the deception plan for 21 Army Group's crossing of the Rhine further south.

On 25 March the Bn was relieved by a Canadian formation and moved over to the eastern sector by BEMMEL in order to provide the firm base for the operations designed to clear the eastern half of the island. The attack met with little opposition and the other two Bdes were soon established along the Rhine.

It was obvious that the next step was to hop across the river and capture Arnhem, and that this task would be one for the Bn. Conferences, plans and changes of plans began to follow each other in rapid succession. The original intention was to cross the river some miles west of Arnhem opposite Wageningen. But this came to nothing as it was decided that the roads required for such a project would not be available. The plan was therefore altered and it was decided to attack Arnhem from the east, involving a crossing of the Issel. The Bn was moved over to a concentration area near Groessen on 9 April, and in spite of the advanced parties being warned that the area was full of mines and booby traps, the move was completed without incident. The next few days were spent in planning and recces. Briefly the plan was that the Glosters should cross first and form a small bridgehead and the Bn and the Essex should then pass through and advance into Arnhem, the town which had baulked the 1 Airborne Div some 7 months previously and which since that date had been fortified by the enemy, and had figured so much in the Bn's thoughts and life during its stay on the "island".

So, on the night of 12 April the Bn loaded itself into "buffaloes" and moved up into the concentration area ready to cross the river. The approach roads were somewhat limited and the traffic control was therefore involved and intricate. However everything moved smoothly, the enemy stonks somehow missed all the Bn's buffaloes, and the night was fine and clear. The preliminary bombardment was heavy and impressive, and although the blowing of the necessary gap in the bund to let the buffaloes through, was bungled, the Glosters were across the river almost on schedule. The Bn. crossed early morning of the 13th and the companies, with "B" Coy in the van, went racing up the roads into the town. Opposition was surprisingly light although there was considerable mortaring and extensive demolitions. The advance through the town went on all day, and although there were not many Bosche about, it was an intricate business and control, amongst all the streets and houses, was difficult. By nightfall the Bn was firmly into the centre of the town, the greater part of which was badly shattered, and we felt that we could not only claim to be the first Bn into Arnhem but also to have helped avenge the Airborne Division.

The following day the Bn spent clearing the western half of the town and was able to see the elaborate defences the enemy had erected, all of which however faced the riverfront. It was clear that Arnhem had been a very pleasant town and one regretted that it had been so hard hit. The capture of ARNHEM marked the end of the Bn's stay on the "island". It had been a long and wearisome period: the continuous contact with the enemy, the severe conditions of floods and weather, and the lack of excitement engendered by the advance, had a cumulative strain which would have affected any but the toughest troops. It was therefore heartening to see that when the Bn was once more called upon to go forward to the attack, it had lost nothing of its old verve and dash.

On the 16th the Bn was suddenly switched eastwards to clear the suburb of Velp. After a preliminary softening up the leading companies supported by tanks moved into the outskirts and were amazed to be greeted by a delirious and overwhelming crowd of civilians. It appeared that the inhabitants of Arnhem had been evacuated to this district and the preliminary artillery shoot had in no way diminished their enthusiasm at seeing their liberators. The few remaining Bosche showed no inclination to fight and the Bn's progress was only made difficult by the swarms of excited children all waving flags, throwing flowers and shouting "good boy Tommy". It was truly an amazing and exhilerating experience and one realised how great was the relief of the Dutch to be freed from their oppressors.

From Velp the Bn was switched back to Arnhem and on the 17th once more set off westwards to contact the retreating enemy. Moving on foot, on lorries and on tanks, the advance developed into what has become to be termed a "swan". During the morning the Bn passed through Osterbeck which bore the signs of the desperate battle which the Airborne troops had waged the previous September; houses were shattered, jeeps, equipment and parachutes lay in tangled heaps, graves were everywhere, and some bodies still remained unburied. It was an impressive memorial to the valour of the 1 Airborne Div and the heroic resistance they offered. Away in the distance lay the remains of the bridge for which they fought in vain and died... The Bn moved on in glorious spring weather through a green and flowering countryside, reminiscent of

England in high summer. The war seemed far away and was only brought home when one of the leading tanks blew up on a minefield. By evening the Bde had secured Wageningen and the Bn was on the high ground NE of the town in surroundings of heather and pine similar to those of Surrey. After a slight readjustment of positions the Bn settled down to shake off the dust of the 15 mile advance and enjoy a nights rest. On the 18th it moved once more to an area just south of Ede to fill in a gap between 56 and 147 Bde. The line now ran almost North and South with the enemy some few miles further west. The weather and surroundings were again idyllic, only marred by the news of the barbaric Hun's threats to blow the Zuider Zee bund.

GERMANY.

On the 24th the unexpected news was received that the Bn was to change its formation yet once more and exchange with a Bn in 53 Division. This news was received with somewhat mixed feelings for many were sorry to leave 56 Bde in which the Bn had been since before "D" day, and in which it had been happy, whilst on the other hand it was pleasing to be going to the Welsh Division which was known to be fighting forward in Germany. The move entailed by this change, was a long one — from west of Arnhem in Holland to Rotenburg in Northern Germany. Fortunately the weather was glorious and in spite of bad roads and a drive of 280 miles, the Bn column arrived at its destination having lost only one vehicle en route — a fine testimony to unit drivers and fitters. The Bn concentrated in a small village called Bothel some 15 miles west of the Elbe, towards which the 7th and Guards Armd Divs were feeling. It was interesting to be at last on German soil; the countryside was green and prosperous, the people were busy tilling the fields and there were few signs either of hostility or of war, save for the numerous white flags fluttering from the farms and houses in the villages.

The Bn had hardly arrived when planning was started for the crossing of the River Elbe. For this operation the Bde was placed under comd of 15 Division who were to make the initial bridgehead. The attack started on 2 May and went without a hitch, in fact so well that the Bn objective was secured by the advanced parties. The journey up to and across the river was slow and laborious, and notable only for two incidents — a short machine gunning by the Luftwaffe which was making a somewhat belated appearance and the singing of a nightingale at 0200 hrs in the morning near a desolated German village in which the Bn column was halted — a small incident which reminded one that even modern war did not altogether disturb the harmony of Nature's way.

Having crossed the river the Bn moved into a small town — Geesthacht — for the capture of which elaborate plans had been prepared, but all to no purpose, as it transpired that this town was a V 2 explosive store, the dangerous nature of which had persuaded the enemy that it were best for them to surrender the village without a fight. From here the Bn moved quickly forward to secure Reinbek and then Ost Börnsen, the latter only some 5 miles from Hamburg. The war was now getting obviously "phoney": telephones were used to ask the village ahead to surrender in order to avoid attacking it, enemy officers came in under a white flag asking for surrender terms, orders had to be given that no fire was to be brought to bear on certain roads in order to allow important enemy envoys to pass through for parleys. Peace was in the air, rumour was rife, hopes ran high. Finally at midnight on 3 May a Brigade conference was held at which orders were given to move into Hamburg at 0530 hrs the following morning. Officially the town had surrendered but no guarantee could be given that the odd S.S. would not fire. The following morning the Bn, having made a special effort to clean itself up, started on the last lap into Hamburg, led by the carriers, "B" Coy and a tp of tanks. The city was found quite lifeless, street after street lined by empty shells of buildings or just a heap of rubble; great stone road blocks barred most of the main roads, but of human life on the streets there was not a sign. Clearing the allotted area was a slow process; arms dumps, prisoners camps and slave workers camps were the main worry. But fortunately the Germans with their doglike sense of discipline were in no way difficult to handle and no sign of disorder interrupted our entry. Strangely enough when the following day the civilians were permitted on the streets, they seemed pleased to see us and displayed neither bitterness nor surliness.

Two days later Germany accepted the terms of unconditional surrender, the war was over and our task completed. To those of the Bn who had landed on "D" day it was the end of a long journey — from the beaches of Arromanches, through France, Belgium, Holland and finally through Germany to Hamburg; and it was no small matter for pride that in spite of these long months and arduous battles the 2/24th ended the campaign in as fine form as they started it, that sunny morning in June nearly a year previously. Although the Bn had been lucky in the final 6 months in having no heavy battles it had undoubtedly done its full share in the first half of the campaign and unfortunately suffered heavily — the total casualties were, killed 7 Offrs 157 ORs., wounded 42 Offrs 542 ORs., missing 2 Offrs 156 ORs. But no victories can be won without cost and the Bn was lucky that the cost was no higher.

And so we leave the Bn amidst the ruins of Hamburg with the old green flag with a white XXIV fluttering in the breeze against a clear blue sky.

And with the campaign over, let it be recorded that the 2/24th did as well as it was expected to do — than which no finer compliment is required.

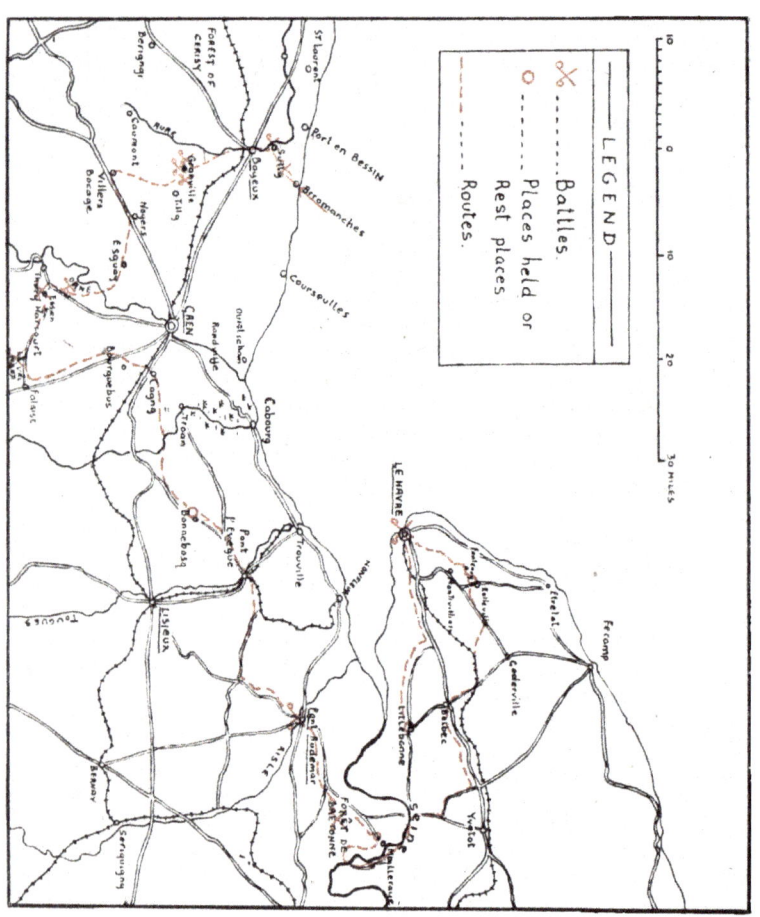

BELGIUM AND HOLLAND

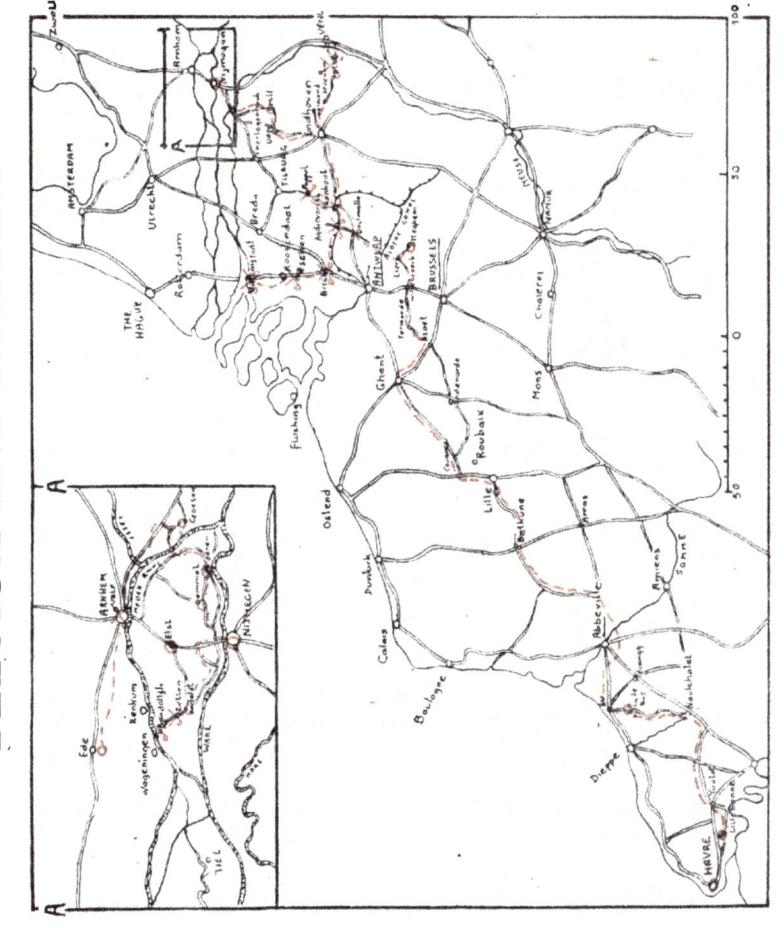

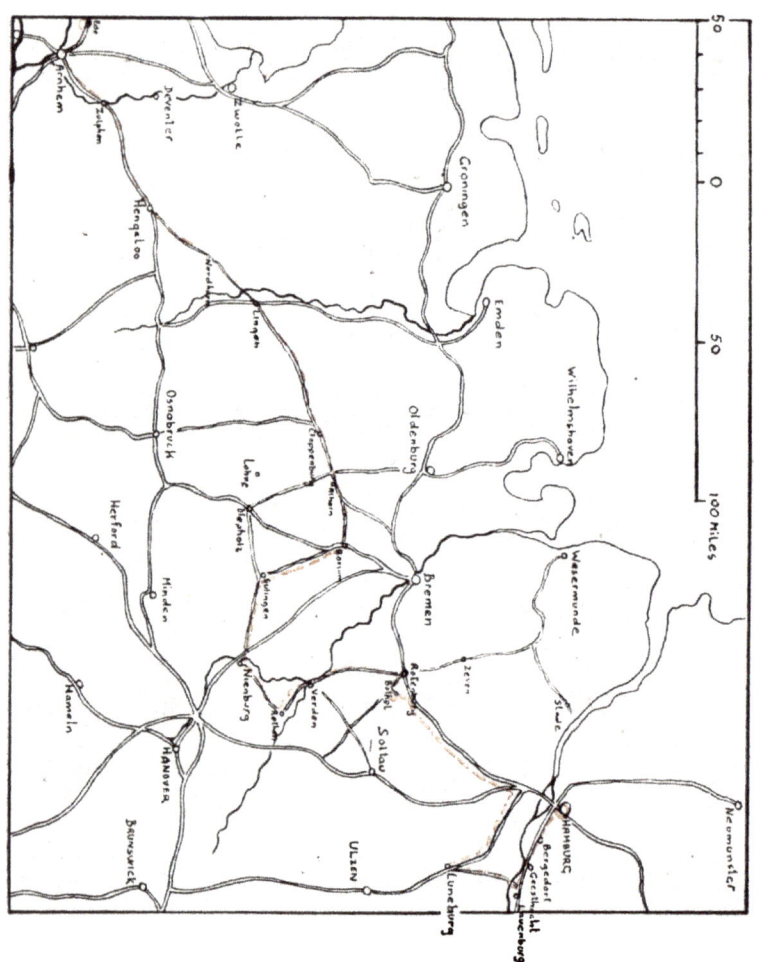

PART II

AN ACCOUNT OF SOME ACTIONS

(1) "D" DAY

The Battalion embarked on 3 American LCsI at LYMINGTON on 3 June and sailed to SOUTHAMPTON, where 4 June was spent on quayside. Everyone was in high spirits. As it grew dusk a spontaneous sing song broke out. Everything was sung from Cwn Rhondda to Eskimo Nell.

It was an unforgettable scene; the clear starlit night, the ships' bridges outlined against the sky, the singers in the dark, a large crowd on the bows who took up the choruses. That night would have been a fitting prelude to "D" Day, but the landing was postponed and another day was spent at SOUTHAMPTON. The Battalion sailed on the evening of the fifth. The weather was cold and windy and showers of rain kept falling. The prudent looked at the swell and took their anti-sea sickness pills. As the LCsI sailed down SOUTHAMPTON WATER a host of ships of every kind could be seen forming up in their places to join the gigantic Armada. A destroyer cheered as the LCsI sailed by and then the coast of HAMPSHIRE and the ISLE OF WIGHT slipped into the darkness.

When dawn broke next morning the coast of FRANCE could still not be seen. A line of ships to port and starboard followed the same course. The sea was rough and the shallow draught LCsI rolled. Many were sick. Cooking was impossible in the galleys and everyone had a cold breakfast. Thro' the clouds above, flights of aircraft were every now and then seen.

The weather cleared a little and at about ten o'clock FRANCE came into sight. In places, clouds of smoke were rising and a few destroyers were shelling the beach in a desultory fashion. The convoy did not, however, land at once but sailed round and round in a circle, two miles from the coast before it received permission. Then the word was given, everyone stood by and the craft made for the shore.

The landing was freakish and typical of combined operations. It took place one mile East of ARROMANCHES, not on any of the planned beaches. Four hundred yards to the left the 2 ESSEX were landing dryshod, but between our LCsI and the shore a channel had formed. A high sea was running and as the troops worked along the life line from the ship to the beach, the waves passed clean over their heads. The smaller ones were out of their depth. Two men only were drowned and the battalion was lucky to get ashore with this small loss of life and no loss of equipment. Everyone was soaked to the skin and the water made the sixty pounds which every man was carrying feel like a ton. Fortunately 231 Bde had done a fine job, the landing was unopposed.

The Battalion had been given several tasks. The most important were as follows. First to occupy the high ground North of BAYEUX. To fulfil this intention it was necessary to carry out other operations. A Radar Station which lay on the road to BAYEUX had to be captured; so had the important bridge over the AVRE at VAUX. Near the bridge there was reported to be a Battery Headquarters. This, too, was an objective. Once over the AVRE, not only had the high ground to the North of BAYEUX to be seized but posts were to be formed at two bridges over a river acting as boundary between the American and British Forces.

It was planned to accomplish these tasks in the following fashion. Immediately on landing all sub units were to move independently to an assembly area three miles inland, near BUHOT. In the assembly area a forward body composed of the carrier platoon, elements of Support Company and "D" Company riding half on the carriers and half on airborne bicycles was to form up and move off ahead of the Battalion. Its task was to carry out all the Battalion intention except the formation of the junction points with the Americans. The rest of the Battalion was to follow as fast as it could on foot.

With one small variation, everything went according to plan. Because the landing had been slower than was expected, the Battalion came ashore in small bodies, not in tactical units and accordingly a preliminary assembly area, only a mile from the beach, was sited and here the Battalion re-organized.

It was strange to be in FRANCE again. The coast looked bare and deserted. In place of crops there were minefields. On every fence hung the skull and cross bones above which was written "ACHTUNG — MINEN" giving a sense of constriction. The country seemed poor and ill kept.

At first there was little to be seen of the enemy except for prisoners, but as the Battalion moved to its assembly area, the road and a village came under mortar fire. A few casualties were inflicted. Under this stimulus sodden packs, which a moment before seemed like lead, became in a second miraculously light. Still more prisoners were taken in the neighbourhood of the assembly area. Snipers and a few Germans holding out with LMGs were encountered.

The forward body moved off down the road without meeting opposition until it reached the RADAR Station, which was held by about four machine gunners. To attack was a difficult problem. The carriers could not deploy off the road because at that time it was believed that every field was mined: one carrier, in fact, blew up on the road. There was no observation to enable the mortars or gunners to fire. There were snipers in the woods around the buildings who hindered reconnaissance. However, "D" company made a right flanking movement and after a little delay the enemy withdrew leaving burning buildings behind them.

It was now growing dark and the forward body pushed boldly on through the narrow lanes without encountering further resistance until it reached VAUX-SUR-AURE. There the bridge was seized and held until the rest of the Battalion came up to consolidate.

What remained of the night passed quietly, except for a few enemy patrols who struck our road blocks. The liveliest encounter occurred when the neighbouring platoons of "A" and "B" companies fired heavily at each other for half an hour. It was an impressive demonstration of the fire power of the platoon tho' fortunately not of the accuracy of our shooting, because no one was hit. Early next morning the Battalion occupied its objective North of BAYEUX.

(2) **SULLY**

Part of the Battalion's "D" Day task had been to establish two junction points with the Americans over a small river running Northwards from BAYEUX to the coast. This had not been accomplished because of the lateness of the landing. On "D" + 1, "A" Company made a reconnaissance in force of the bridge at SULLY where they encountered stiff resistance and withdrew after fighting a sharp action. There was no sign of the 1st American Division, who, it was afterwards learnt had been held up by very heavy fighting on the beaches. On "D" + 2 it was decided to help the American advance by capturing the bridge and chateau of SULLY.

SULLY is a little village in a valley, built around a bridge over the river. On the East a road runs parallel to the river two hundred yards from the river bank. Four hundred yards further East a second road runs parallel to the first. The village is approached from the East by another road cutting the lateral roads at right angles. On the right of the bridge are fields with banks and thick hedgerows; to the left are houses. To reach the chateau which stands on the Western side of the valley it is necessary to cross the bridge and turn to the left. The country is very close. The roads are lined with tall trees and every field is bordered with steep banks and hedges.

For support in the attack the Battalion was given one field regiment, a medium regiment, a platoon of 4.2 Mortars, two troops of tanks and a cruiser. The plan was for "A" Company to make a firm base in the area of the Forming up Point and for "B" Company to pass through and capture all of the village on the Eastern bank. "A" Company was then to move through "B" Company and take the chateau. The artillery was to put down concentrations upon the cross roads, the area of the bridge and upon the chateau. The tanks were to give covering fire from the right flank. It was impossible to see the objective because of the close country and snipers. It was thought that "A" Company might have to fight to reach the F. U. P. There was not time to patrol.

The attack went in at 1215 hours. It was found that the cruiser could not fire because no satisfactory observation could be obtained. The tanks in the same way could find no position to give covering fire. The F. U. P. which was chosen from the map, turned out to be entirely exposed on the left flank. As time was short, "A" Company could not clear the area and "B" Company were therefore unable to deploy into assault formation, but had to remain on the road. The artillery came down in a heavy concentration on the first cross roads, which were heavily wooded; in consequence many shells burst short and "B" Company had to go forward in their own concentration. Finally, because there had been no reconnaissance and the operation was hurried, one platoon commander missed his way and instead of taking a track round to the right of the village, continued down the central road. However, the attack went in.

Opposition was met from some houses near the first cross roads. An enemy MG fired at the leading troops but was forced to withdraw by a determined section attack. The assault continued until on the edge of the village, the company was held up by a body of enemy an 8.8 mm gun and a 2 cm Flak gun. The position was critical. The only cover available was the road which was sheltered by high banks, but being the obvious approach, the road became a target for mortars and grenades. The company then split into two parts. One under the 2IC tried to get forward, while the other, under the Company Commander worked round the right flank and got behind the enemy position. The enemy seeing that they were outflanked, withdrew at the double, hotly pursued. The troops were now fighting with great confidence. Again the company broke into two and while one party cleaned up the houses and hedgerows, the other made a magnificent dash across the open bridge, gained the otherside and formed a bridgehead.

"A" Company now passed through and swinging left attacked the chateau with two platoons on the left and one on the right. The attack encountered stiff opposition. The chateau, which afterwards turned out to be a Brigade Headquarters, was strongly defended. It was ringed with wire. Underneath the chateau were dugouts 30 ft deep from which radiated underground passages to posts around the perimeter. In addition, there was a system of well sited slit trenches. Dummy tanks were erected in the grounds. "A"Company reinforced by one platoon of "B" Company fought extremely well. Although subjected to heavy fire by an enemy who knew every inch of the ground, they worked steadily forward through the orchards which surround the chateau. They could not, however, get to assaulting distance and the tanks who were operating in support were handicapped by the close country and the presence of two more 8.8 mm guns. It was a very bitter fierce contest.

While the fighting was going on, another complication arose. The Americans were pushing down the West bank of the river driving the enemy before them and though they were still some way off, these withdrawing detachments threatened to take our attacking companies in the rear. A Platoon was put out to form a firm base but before it could dig in or get anti-tank guns up, an enemy S. P. gun appeared and from short range blasted it out of position. The S. P. gun came forward and temporarily dominated the bridge, cutting off "A" Company and advanced Bn HQ from the rest of the Battalion and also destroying three carriers.

The situation was critical. The company was unable to get nearer the chateau and was being counter attacked, while at the rear, this new threat was developing. It was impossible to reinforce the attack because the remainder of the Battalion was back at BAYEUX still holding the defensive position. Therefore, the decision to withdraw was made and all the troops across the river came back under cover of smoke put down by the artillery. "C" Company was brought up from BAYEUX and held the village to the East of the river all that night. In the morning, patrols reported that the enemy had withdrawn, and so, though the chateau was not taken in its effects, the attack was successful and the advancing Americans did not find a strongly held position to hold up their progress.

There were many gallant actions performed during this battle. When a platoon was withdrawing down a sunken lane, with the enemy on either side, sniping and throwing grenades, one platoon sergeant showed complete contempt of danger, walking up and down his platoon encouraging the men and hurling back Mills grenades. Though seriously wounded himself he got back to our lines. A private soldier seeing two men hit as they tried to cross the gap and the rest hang back hesitating to cross, at once jumped into the open and firing his Bren gun, though totally exposed, covered them all across. A stretcher-bearer fearlessly brought in the wounded under fire, crawling up to collect them from the forward platoons.

The battle of SULLY was a small action compared with those in which the Battalion afterwards took part, but it was the Battalion's first serious attack since "D" Day. The shortness and the setting of the battle gave it a drama often lacking in larger operations. It was there, that the Battalion first proved it could fight well and therefore SULLY occupies an unique place in the story of events since "D" Day.

(3) GRANVILLE TO ST. GERMAIN D'ECTOT

By the beginning of July the bridgehead had been slightly extended, and while the build up for a break through continued inside, the formations on the perimeter kept up a series of containing attacks. 30 Corps was holding a line roughly North of the TILLY — CAUMONT road. In this line an enemy salient bulged North to GRANVILLE, a little village about four kilometres North of ST. GERMAIN D'ECTOT. 56 Brigade was ordered to push in this salient. The 2 ESSEX were ordered to attack on the left and 2 SWB on the right.

The Battalion positions were along a ridge of high ground at LA BUTTE. Through the middle of this position a road ran due South to GRANVILLE in the bottom of a valley and leaving the BOIS DE ST. GERMAIN on the left crossed the TILLY road at LA CHAPELLE cross roads, continuing to ST. GERMAIN D'ECTOT in the distance. The countryside was very close.

The fields were bounded by thick hedgerows and high earth banks. LA BUTTE and GRANVILLE were surrounded by orchards. As usual, it was most difficult to get good observation. In fact, as was afterwards discovered, the Germans were the only people to have good O. Ps. in the area of LA CHAPELLE cross roads. Beyond GRANVILLE lay the BOIS DE ST. GERMAIN, a large, dense wood to which everyone took an instinctive dislike.

The battle of GRANVILLE falls into three phases. First, the attack on LA CHAPELLE cross roads. Second, after the partial success of the attack, the gradual penetration forward to the line of the TILLY road. Third, the attack on the ST. GERMAIN D'ECTOT feature.

For a week before the attack the enemy positions were continuously patrolled. It was possible to piece together some idea of the enemy's dispositions. On one of these patrols, an officer was shot three times in the leg and wounded by grenade splinters and yet after lying out for three days eventually managed to crawl back into our lines, a wonderful example of determination. One difficulty encountered by patrols was that the enemy territory was riddled with alternative positions amongst which the Germans frequently moved.

The Battalion was given what appeared to be overwhelming support. The Divisional artillery and three battalions of American artillery, a platoon of 4.2. mortars, two MMG pls, 1 Sqn 4/7 D Gs (Sherman Tanks), one 17 pdr tp, 1 tp of flails (Westminster Dragoons) 1 sec Fd Sqn RE, 1 tp of AVRE'S and one tp of Crocodiles (Flame throwers).

The plan in brief was to attack with two companies, one on each side of the road to GRANVILLE, with the orchards on the line of the TILLY road as objective. The sec of RE were to clear the central road of mines, and the flails to flail a shallow track up to the objective. Two troops of tanks were to support each company and the remainder of the supporting arms were to remain in reserve. The Arty and mortars fired on targets chosen from the map and patrols reports.

The attack went in at 0800 hours. On the right "C" Coy pushed on through heavy mortar fire and crossed the lateral road running through GRANVILLE and were then held up by Spandau fire from an orchard. The tanks were delayed by a minefield and it took sometime for them to work through and help "C" Coy to get on. On the left, "A" Coy advanced through the same heavy defensive fire up to GRANVILLE and there encountered Spandau fire from a strong point sited on the edge of the BOIS DE ST. GERMAIN. An AVRE sent to help them went up on a mine. The banks acted as antitank obstacles and prevented effective tank support. "A" Coy were definitely stuck. "C" Coy commander was wounded by a Schmeisser bullet; the firer pretended to surrender and then fired again. He was knocked into a slit trench with a grenade as company. Under their 2 IC, "C" company reached their objective with a third of their strength left, after pushing through heavy mortar and shell fire. "D" Company were pushed up behind them and began to dig in.

Since any further advance was impossible on the left owing to the strong point at the North of the BOIS DE ST. GERMAIN, "B" company was ordered to attack the South of the BOIS passing through "D" Coy. A troop of tanks was given the task of guarding their right flank.

As "B" Coy formed up to attack, very heavy fire came down on them and at this moment the Germans put in a perfect counterattack, made by tanks and infantry. "B" and "D" company were forced back and the situation was extremely dangerous. OC "D" coy acted with great decision and the two companies reformed around him.

Fighting throughout was very fierce. A NCO of "D" Coy stalked and disabled a Mk IV with a piat. An 8.8 mm had caused heavy casualties in "D" coy and the company swore to get it. They worked forward and shot up the crew, capturing the gun, which unfortunately was later retaken by the enemy.

It was now late in the evening. Before it became dark, "B" and "D" coys withdrew slightly and took up defensive positions. The remnants of "C" Coy joined "A" Coy who with the carriers held the former battalion area. As soon as it was night, enemy patrols pressed forward firing tracer from their Spandaus. The situation was very precarious. The Battalion had suffered 180 casualties nearly all of them in rifle coys, and with four weak companies were holding a lozenge shaped position, nearly half a mile long with two companies at each end. In between, the enemy could freely infiltrate, and rations could not be got forward.

Next morning, the two forward companies, who were only fifty yards from the enemy, were counter-attacked by tanks and one platoon was overrun. The remainder held.

So ended the first phase of the battle. The objectives were not gained but the intention was fulfilled. Our attack and that of the 2 ESSEX on the left wiped out two enemy battalions and forced the enemy to remove a third reserve bn from HOTTOT, which 231 Bde was to attack two days later. By actions such as these all along the front the Germans were prevented from pulling out formations and building up a concentrated force.

There followed ten difficult days. The forward companies were in close contact with the enemy, they were overlooked and their positions were registered.

All NORMANDY was full of dead cows but this little area seemed especially full of dead horses and cattle, the stench was indescribable. Snipers crept up and tried to pick off careless men. One German was shot 20 yards from an antitank gun; in his hands were six stick grenades tied together.

The tension after the stress of a hard fight caused many exhaustion cases and the sight of these unfortunate men trembling and crying made the problem of morale even more difficult. "Barking Dogs", the German rocket bomb which when discharged makes a harsh rasping sound like a dog's bark made their first appearance. All the time communication with the rest of the battalion was dangerous. However, the companies held and fought back.

It was decided that the orchard at LA CHAPELLE was the key to the enemy position and an 20 July after three previous attempts a "C" Coy patrol, with artillery support, got into the orchard and though mortared dug themselves in. "C" Coy followed them; "A" Coy beat through the BOIS DE ST. GERMAIN and the whole battalion was stepped up to the line of the TILLY road. Everything was ready for the next stage of the battle.

Before passing on, it is worth while saying a few words about the German positions at LA CHAPELLE. The enemy had correctly appreciated it as the vital ground. It was protected by a big dog-leg minefield of Teller mines laid in unusual density. Behind were infantry positions beautifully dug, making use of the sunken lanes as communicating trenches. Near these were dugouts made habitable in the German tradition of comfort in the field, by loot from neighbouring French houses. On top was a position protected by wire, and in front and along a covered approach, a large field of mustard pot anti-personnel mines. These alone, even after the position was taken, wounded one company commander, and a RE officer and sergeant. The side roads had mines in the road so skilfully concealed that a German tank went up on them. The BOIS DE ST. GERMAIN on the flank was mined and protected in the same way. It was a model defensive position and from the top there was the best O. P. we had so far encountered in NORMANDY.

On 31 July the battalion once more attacked. The objective was ST. GERMAIN D'ECTOT ridge, a long feature upon which the village sat.

From our own patrols it was known that 2 Pz Div had been relieved by 231 Div who were of lower fighting quality. The Intelligence, that Fairy Wishful Thinking of the Army, said the enemy was weak and would withdraw without fighting. It was unfortunate the battalion had to attack over ground which had not been included in its patrol boundaries.

The country was the same as around GRANVILLE, being close and wooded. Along the top of the ridge ran a series of orchards. The battalion had a considerable amount of artillery in support, which because of Intelligence reports did not fire on the positions, where enemy were ultimately found but started — well behind them. It also had one tp and half Sqn HQ of a Sqn of the 13/18 Hussars, one tp Flails and 1 tp of Flame Throwers.

Because the frontage was narrow, the attack was made with one company up. Owing to the country, it was only possible to see objectives off the map. "C" Coy was given the task of clearing an orchard at LA COUARDE and then occupying the right hand orchard on the ridge. They went into the attack supported by 1 tp of tanks. The flame throwers were suffering from a mechanical breakdown. Moving, perhaps incautiously, across a field "C" Coy were fired on by Spandaus at a range of three hundred yards. They made every effort to get on but were pinned down and disorganized. Once again, the enemy were showing anything but disinclination to fight.

It was decided to put "B" Coy in to retrieve the situation. This time the coy commander wisely took his time over the reconnaissance. He arranged his plan with the tanks and at 1600 hours went into the attack. When fired on, the company executed a perfect left flanking and supported by the tanks, who went fearlessly forward shooting at anything they could see, chased the enemy clean out of his positions. One section commander even led his section into the assault; bayonets fixed, five yards between men as was done in 1914—18, a very rare sight in this war. "B" Coy got their objective and "D" Coy was passed through to take the orchard to their left. The flails flailed a path for the crocodiles up to the ridge, who squirted flame into the orchard which the company took without a casualty.

Three companies were now established on the ridge but ST. GERMAIN D'ECTOT had still not been attacked. It was, therefore, planned that "D" Coy supported by Flails, AVRE's and Crocodiles should capture the village next morning.

At 0830 hours the attack went in. A large village can be a difficult place to capture if the enemy fight it out. "D" Coy was weak in men and ST. GERMAIN D'ECTOT was a sizeable place. It was an anxious moment. Fortunately the attack went like a demonstration. The artillery fired and the flails beat a path to the edge of the houses. The AVRE'S fired their dust-bins at a few likely buildings, which disappeared with a fearful crash and cloud of smoke. The Crocodiles belched out a frightful sheet of flame and "D" Coy charged through like demons. It has not been established how many enemy there were in ST. GERMAIN. Someone saw a platoon rushing away as if the devil were on their tails, but apart from a brief burst of Spandau fire, no more opposition was met.

The battalion at once dug in on the ridge and next morning pushed forward to occupy the LAUNAY ridge above CANDON. No resistance was met. It was there learnt that the enemy had been forming up to counter attack ST. GERMAIN D'ECTOT when the 90 Fd Regt put a concentration beyond the village and hit them, discouraging further efforts.

From now on the German withdrawal to the FALAISE pocket began and the battalion moved to a new area.

(4) LE VAL WOOD

On 17 August 44, 56 Brigade moved from the river ORNE and took over a position from 53 Div about 6 miles SW of FALAISE, on the Northern edge of the FALAISE pocket. The brigadier was not entirely satisfied with the lay out and the brigade began to edge forward with the intention of squeezing out the enemy trapped in the pocket. "A" Coy moved forward a mile to pt 231 and during the night 17/18 August "B" and "D" coys worked forward a further three quarters of a mile in front of "A" Coy. While on their objective, "B" Coy heard sounds of digging from LE VAL wood to their left.

LE VAL wood is a small wood on a hill just SE of the hamlet of LE VAL. It dominates the slopes beneath it, but it is hard to observe except from a position on the left flank which was not discovered until late in the day. Beneath it runs a small stream and the road through the hamlet lies to its West. It was masked from our own positions.

When it was light, "B" Coy were fired on from the wood. A patrol was sent in but driven back by heavy Spandau fire. A company attack was put in. After a heavy artillery concentration "B" coy attacked the North of the wood with two platoons. They reached the edge but at least six spandaus opened up on them from dug in positions and they could make no further progress. The coy commander withdrew one platoon and together with the reserve platoon attacked again from the West. Once more the forces reached the edge of the wood but could not penetrate. The company then withdrew.

This bald account hardly does justice to the gallant efforts of "B" coy, who were below strength and tired by previous fighting, and a night without sleep. They were attacking a numerically superior force dug in on ground of its own choosing, without any support except a preliminary artillery concentration. They fought with dash and bravery. One private in a section which had reached the objective saw the rest of his platoon held up by machine gun and rifle fire. He noticed also a German helmet bob up near to him. He at once dashed over, pulled the rifle out of the German's hands and made him prisoner; further on he seized a machine gun by the muzzle with his bare hands and took the crew prisoner. He was then shot in the leg but continued to guard the prisoners until the rest of his platoon came up.

"B" Coy was withdrawn and since there was no urgent necessity to capture the wood, other means were tried. During the day, the enemy shelled and mortared the battalion. However, at 2200 hours, the Corps artillery put down a concentration on the wood using the "time on target method" so that approximately 144 25 lb shells and 32 100 lb shells hit the wood at the same time. It was an impressive crump. "A" and "C" coys at once put in fighting patrols but the enemy still drove them out. Prisoners taken by these patrols reported that there were about 80 men of different units at LE VAL and that they had no real organisation.

Next morning, a battalion attack was made supported by artillery. "A" and "C" Coys came in from the left flank; "B" Coy acted as cut off and "D" Coy were in reserve. The attack was a complete success, and the enemy surrendered. Thirty three more prisoners were taken, which with the killed and wounded account for most of the original eighty.

A disagreeable part of the battle was the number of civilians killed and wounded in the village, largely caused by the Germans taking the civilian's shelters for their own use. Though LE VAL was a small action it brings out two lessons. First, that the disorganized army can fight very well. At this time the Press was glibly saying that all organized resistance had ended in the FALAISE pocket. Second, that woods held by determined enemy are formidable objectives.

(5) PONT AUDEMER

49 Div with the remainder of 1 British Corps in the 1st Canadian Army were pressing towards the SEINE, crossing the lesser rivers which run parallel with it to the sea. 2 ESSEX had formed a bridgehead over the River CALONNE at COUR-MEILLES, through which the battalion passed, moving with a forward body in front, until PONT AUDEMER on the River RISLE was reached. There the bridges had been blown and the far bank was held by enemy rearguards. All attempts by the 6 Airborne Div to get across by day had failed. Movement in the open brought down mortar and artillery fire, because the enemy had excellent observation. 56 Brigade was ordered to cross and establish a bridgehead. The battalion was given the task of crossing in the area of the town.

At PONT AUDEMER the RISLE valley is broad and steep. To the East of the town steep, heavily wooded and in some parts, precipitous cliffs rise up. On these, houses and hotels are built where the ground is suitable. The cliffs are broken by a valley and road which runs Westward into the centre of the town. On the East, the country rises more slowly in heavily wooded slopes to a height of three hundred feet. PONT AUDEMER is a pretty little town cut in two by the river, with coloured roofs, churches and green fields. The river runs through the built up area and is flanked by houses, shops and warehouses.

For all its attractiveness, PONT AUDEMER was not a healthy place. It was regularly shelled and anyone who exposed himself to the far bank was sniped at. However, it was imperative to find a crossing place over the river which appeared to run too swiftly for assault boats, and the C. O. decided to make use of local knowledge. The F.F.I. were therefore contacted at their HQ. This was a large hall, filled with men wearing the red, white and blue armband and cross of LORRAINE. They were prolific of contradictory advice. The majority had a healthy respect for the river line, but in the end one voluntered to lead a reconnaissance party, whom he took along a tortuous route through offices, under desks, in shops, in and out of a tannery until he finally brought them to a building a few yards from the river's edge.

Here, he said, the water was only four feet deep. It was impossible to test it as the crossing was completely exposed and movement would have jeopardized surprise.

At the schools they say an opposed river crossing takes at least four days to plan. At PONT AUDEMER orders were finished at 2030 hours and the leading company went into the attack at 2230 hours. A Tac HQ was put into the town and the axis from the Tac HQ to the crossing marked by tape. The companies collected in assembly areas in the rear. "B" Coy went into the attack at 2230 hours and moving in single file along the extraordinary route reconnoitred before hand, went across the river. The point of crossing was a surprise and they met with little opposition. "A" Company followed. It was no ordinary test of discipline to wade across a swift flowing stream in the pitch darkness, carrying one's arms above one's head and then strike out through unreconnoitred buildings to scale the steep cliffs beyond. However, both companies got on to their objectives. There were only twelve casualties. A voice called out in French from a house and when a section advanced not expecting trouble, it met a burst of machine gun fire. The success of the operation can in some part be attributed to the excellence of the communications. Tac and Main HQ and the assembly area were in perfect touch all the time and behind each assaulting company moved a signal detachment unreeling line.

When it grew light, the two forward companies were cut off from the rest of the battalion by enemy still remaining in the town, but if their position was uncomfortable, that of the enemy was far worse, because they were a rearguard whose line of withdrawal was threatened. A company sentry looking down into the valley, spotted enemy transport and a sentry standing in a gap with a Spandau at his feet. The coy commander concentrated five Bren guns and opened fire at 700x. The sentry fell and each time the enemy came out to pick up the gun and bring in the bodies, he was fired on again and suffered some loss.

In the afternoon, the enemy began to withdraw under the threat of 147 Bde who were working up the East bank of the river from the South. "D" coy crossed over and the battalion concentrated for its next move forward.

After the battle, when all has gone well and the position is taken and casualties are few, there is a temptation to say "There was nothing in it after all". PONT AUDEMER was a success, but it was not an easy operation. If a dangerous reconnaissance had not been carried out, if the company commanders had got flurried because of the little time for preparation, if the troops had lost their heads in the water, it would have been a failure, and no one would have got across. In fact, no other battalion did. A day's delay at least would have occurred when speed in pursuit of the enemy was vital. None of these things happened, because the battalion was efficient and above all determined.

(6) LE HAVRE

At the beginning of September the battalion crossed the SEINE and took part in the attack on LE HAVRE. As they retreated at full speed Northwards, the Germans had left considerable garrisons in most of the important coastal towns. Their object was to tie down large forces of British Troops in reducing these places and also to deny to the advancing army bases which would shorten their lines of communication. From the British point of view, it was vital to capture a large port, and the more quickly it could be done the sooner troops would be released for other tasks and the less time would the Germans have for extensive demolitions. LE HAVRE was accordingly invested.

The 49 and 51 Divs were selected for the job. Both divisions encircled the port, pushing in until they made contact with the enemy on the high ground surrounding the town. LE HAVRE was ringed with troops and guns. A great amount of artillery was deployed. Regiments of field, medium and heavy guns surrounded it on all sides.

It was a wonderful sight at night to see the whole sky flickering with the flashes of guns and the dull glow of fires burning in the stricken town. Besides the artillery, the RAF took a hand, for four days, culminating in a terrific raid on the day before the attack. Lancasters came slowly wheeling over and dropped thousands of tons of incendiaries on the German defences.

Very full information from deserters and F.F.I. was obtained about the German fortifications. They were considerable, consisting of a ring of concrete strong points on the high ground above the town, strengthened by extensive mine fields, anti-tank ditches and wire fences. In the town itself were two large forts and in the docks every type of defensive position known to human ingenuity, most of them, luckily, facing seawards.

The plan of attack was that all formations should converge simultaneously on the town but as a preliminary, two dominating hills to the NE of the town had to be seized, otherwise the other attacks could not get forward. The task of taking these features was given to 56 Bde. The battalion's objective was the right hand hill, which contained three woods, one behind the other. In each wood were deep concrete dug-outs and fortifications. The position was enfiladed by a fourth wood, about which some anxiety was felt.

After a heavy preliminary bombardment and Typhoon strafe, the battalion went into the attack on the evening of Sat. 2 September.

First went the Flails with the task of breaching the minefield. They were followed by AVRE'S equipped to deal with the anti-tank ditch and pillboxes. The tank sqn followed and finally, for once, came the infantry.

The attack was made over open downland. In front of the enemy positions was a steep little valley, ideal for DF fire. As the tanks appeared, they were engaged by two 8.8 mm firing from the wood on the flank. They were in concrete cupolas and very difficult to silence. The infantry began to cross the gully and down came the DF fire. It only caught the rear of "D" coy, who gallantly dashed forward through the minefield, over the wire and on to the first objective. Jumping down the concrete dug-out, they found forty Germans; only a few of the enemy manned the slit trenches.

"A" Coy now had the task of passing through "D" but the defensive fire fell in the middle of the company, completely disorganizing it. Heavy fire also came from the locality on the flank. Only the company commander and a section reached their objective. OC "B" Coy seeing that "A" coy had insufficient men to capture the second wood, cleverly led his men round to the left flank avoiding the enemy DF, mopped up the second objective and then supported by flame throwers, swept into the third wood and cleared it of enemy.

All objectives were captured. Only small bodies of enemy showed fight, but as in many attacks, the real enemy was not the infantry soldier but enemy artillery. Once the battalion were through the defensive fire and on to the objectives, and this required guts and steadiness, the positions were taken. The enemy defences showed true German thoroughness. Each had a dug-out thirty feet deep, with concrete steps and steel doors. Down below were fans for air conditioning, sleeping rooms, armouries, concrete O. Ps. and stacks of food. Many dugouts connected up to slit trenches. In fact so excellent were the fortifications, that though they were heavily shelled during the night by the Germans, the companies occupying them did not sustain one casualty.

Innumerable prisoners were taken. It was an operation in which no really accurate count could be kept. Amongst them was one of those queer phenomena, the officer who shouts out that he wants to die for Hitler but has apparently neglected to take the opportunity while the fighting was on. A section rushing into an O.P. caught an F.O.O. as he gave fire orders over the telephone to his guns. A platoon runner walking through the woods in the dark with a message, saw six Germans creeping down a trench towards coy HQ. He stalked them and charged with bayonet fixed. They all surrendered.

Next day the battalion moved down into the outskirts of LE HAVRE, mopping up small bodies as they went. Though the enemy was not resisting desperately, it was trying fighting moving through minefields and wondering whether one would go up, searching the houses, routing out snipers and expecting at every street corner a burst of machine gun fire.

On Mon 4 September, the advance continued through the town down to the docks. The F.F.I. co-operated, pointing out enemy positions and taking the prisoners off our hands. There seemed more prisoners than attacking troops. All day long field-grey columns went by through the crowds of jeering French. About 1030 hours it was all over. The commander of LE HAVRE was a prisoner, a cold disapproving figure trying to look dignified with his batman and staff on top of a Honey; white flags were appearing in the harbour; the enormous forts and pillboxes were giving up. Only a few little posts held out and they were soon dealt with. By 1900 hours LE HAVRE was ours.

The papers said that LE HAVRE was an easy battle. It was for two reasons. First, it was a well planned operation. The capture of LE HAVRE must go down in military history as a classic attack on a town. Second, when the situation was critical, our troops were willing to risk more and give more than the enemy. The 2/24th came out of the battle with enhanced prestige. It took the toughest enemy position in the first assault and it was the first battalion to drive through the town and reach the sea.

It was no mean achievement to capture in a 36 hours attack a great port with a population of over 100,000 to take 13,000 prisoners and overcome defences which the enemy had for four years prepared. In short, LE HAVRE was a great victory to which the 2/24th made a glorious contribution.

(7) FIGHTING PATROL

The patrol flopped down on the ground. Fifteen minutes to wait! A few went to sleep, the rest sat testing their weapons and thinking. The sombre BOIS DE ST. GERMAIN encompassed them, a dark, thick wood smelling of rotten vegetation and death, where the rides were rutted by tanks and bordered by trip wires. The trees were smashed by gunfire and the shell craters gave off a sharp, acrid smell. A pale moon obscured by flying clouds shone with a fitful light. Away to the right three aircraft flares floated slowly to the ground. The occasional crump and whine of shells broke the silence.

Hell! Thought the officer, what a party! What were they doing now in Montreal? Would he ever see it again? Still, he was glad to be here. He had a score to settle since a few days ago two of the company had been cut in half by a mine. The boys thought the same. He looked at his men. Nine stocky figures, faces blackened, cap comforters on head, sprawling on the mud. I could do with a pint, Pte Jones said to himself, a bloody, old pint with froth on the top. What a fool to volunteer for patrol, because some old bastard wanted a prisoner! Still, it meant three days by the sea in the rest camp if they got one. Someone had to do it. DUW! DUW! he went to sleep. The sergeant patted his rifle. No stens for him, not since one jammed at a bad moment. He tested the bayonet. This was like going into the ring, only there wasn't a referee. So they wanted a prisoner; he'd get one if he had to put a ring through his nose "Time" said the officer and the patrol got to its feet.

They moved off from the headquarters where they had been waiting, and followed the guide up to an outpost which was to be their patrol base. As they went along the rough tracks and crossed the road, the air was full of the menace of mortar bombs and shells, that paralysing threat which makes you plan your course from ditch to ditch and slit trench to slit trench. At the outpost they halted. The patrol officer and F.O.O. dropped off into a disused enemy mortar pit. In front was No Man's land.

Punctually, at 2330 hours the artillery support began. The guns were firing into enemy positions, three hundred yards behind the selected enemy post. Four minutes fire, three minutes silence, more fire, more silence, so it went on for half an hour.

Under the cover of the sound, the patrol moved forward in two parties, led by the officer. It worked along the hedgerows, slowly, cautiously waiting for a crump of shells to cover the noise made by breaking through hedges which held up its progress. A sound was heard to the left. Everyone froze. Two men crawled away into the darkness to investigate. They came back ten minutes later and reported they could see no enemy. On went the patrol, moving more cautiously than ever because the enemy were within 150 yards. A wind rose up and it began to rain. The moon was obscured by cloud. Thank God! Thought everyone. Behind them they heard explosions, as the enemy roused by the artillery fire put down his DF at midnight, our own artillery stopped firing. The patrol was on its own.

Everything was deathly silent, except on the right where a Bren fired a few bursts. They lay still and listened, hoping that the enemy, notoriously talkative at night might give away his position. Not a sound was heard.

Then in a split second, it broke. Brrrrh — Brrrrh! From thirty yards away a spandau fired two long whirring bursts at the leading men. It was the gunner's death warrant, signed by himself. The patrol lay flat; they knew the drill. Swiftly, silently the Bren groups moved over to the right of the field. Tho bayonet men formed up on the left, bayonets fixed, ready to go in. Suddenly, the Brens opened up with their steady, reassuring plop firing long bursts at the flash of the enemy automatics. On the right, the Sergeant waited. When he judged the moment ripe, he shouted "Charge!" deceiving the enemy as to the direction of the attack. At the same time, filled with a primeval fury inherited from Heaven knows what wild ancestors, he rushed forward at the enemy trench. He reached it just before the assaulting troops, leapt down where three Germans lay dead, seized a fourth wounded man, and shouting "Get up! Get up!" threw him over his shoulder and doubled back two hundred yards towards our own lines, carrying his burden.

Back in patrol base, they had been trying to follow the course of the battle. They heard the artillery support come down, then the silence, followed by the Spandau fire. Again there was silence, then fire from the Bren, a shout and at last the green verey light, signal to cover the withdrawal. Tho F.O.O., in the calm way of gunners took his microphone, "Lost, I say again, lost", he said. In a few seconds the air was filled with the whine of shells sealing off the patrol from pursuit. In front of the mortar pit the sound of running feet was heard and dark forms came out of the night. "D" coy patrol", they whispered. "Did you get one?" "Of course!"

Back at coy HQ they put the bleeding, unconscious form on an ambulance jeep and drove him back over the bumpy tracks, through the wood to the RAP. He died without regaining consciousness. In his pockets were photographs of himself as a member of the Hitler Jugend, in the Arbeitsdienst, in the Wehrmacht. Trained as a soldier since he was ten, he died the death for which he was prepared.

His pay book went back by special DR to brigade. It showed that 231 Div had relieved 2 Pz Div in the line; back went the news from brigade to division, from division to corps and so to Army, and from there to levels incomprehensible save to the elect.

"Sounds as if your chaps had a good party last night, can I see them"? said the Brigade Major; but the chaps, assisted by a lot of Calvados were asleep, conscious of a job well done.

(8) THE "ISLAND".

Days spent on the "island" in whichever sector it might be — were all very similar — active patrolling, occasional "stonking", continuous "stag" and watery foxholes or cellars. Periodic clashes with enemy patrols added excitement to this otherwise rather boring routine of a defensive position, in the finer arts of which the Bn became well skilled. Perhaps a description of the Bn's occupation of the ZETTEN sector can be taken as representative of our activities on this front.

On 20 December the Bn took over the defence of the ZETTEN sector, which was in process of minor re-organisation owing to rising flood water. On taking over it was apparent that the forward company area — "A" Coy — was fast becoming untenable as it was separated from the remainder of the Bn by a stretch of water 6 ft deep (and still rising) and could only be maintained by "DUKW". Therefore, it was decided to withdraw this company and hold the sector with two companies up — on the dry ground 500 yds South of ZETTEN — with a semi-circle of four standing patrols out ahead on the outskirts of the village to watch and guard its exits. Although this entailed surrendering observation of the northern approaches into ZETTEN, it had the advantage of preventing the enemy observing our own positions, which he could only approach through the water in boats.

It was during the process of withdrawing "A" Coy that the first clash with the enemy on this sector occurred. Two "dukws" had just withdrawn the forward platoon and most of the reserve ammunition, when out of the mist loomed three boat loads of Germans. Visibility being no more than 20 yards, it was not until the enemy had started creeping up from the rear on Coy HQ that they were spotted. A close quarter fire fight ensued with the enemy dodging in and out of the houses. After half an hour of this, however, they had had enough and pulled out, leaving behind five dead — of which one was the commanding officer of a parachute battalion, a valuable identification — and one prisoner.

This clash was typical of many which the standing patrols had on the succeeding days. Enemy patrols would come forward with little caution, bump our patrols and invariably be forced to withdraw with loss. In fact it became evident from captured patrol reports, that few of his patrolmen were ever getting back. As an example, on 1 January, out of one enemy patrol of 5 men, 4 were killed or captured. It also was learnt from these documents that the enemy appreciated that we were holding the village with a complete company, and it was to locate this coy's positions prior to launching an attack that was the object of his patrolling. It speaks well for our patrols that although they were completely isolated from the remainder of the Bn and often surrounded by water and shrouded in mist, not one was definitely pinpointed by the enemy and not once did any clash result in favour to the enemy. This was only made possible by the patrols always holding their fire until they could be sure of accounting for every man in the enemy patrol — a fine testimony to their cool courage and discipline.

At the same time nightly patrols were sent out from the Bn's lines to contact the enemy. Owing to the floods these patrols had to employ the somewhat unorthodox method of paddling forward in assault boats. And sitting in a flimsy assault boat with water lapping all around and with strong currents sweeping the boat suddenly off its course, undoubtedly added to the strain of the always nerve-racking business of patrolling in enemy territory.

Knowing that the enemy was intending to attack the ZETTEN positions, it was decided to upset his calculations by staging a counter-raid against the "Castle".

The "Castle" was a strongly built square stone mansion surrounded by a moat full of water across which was only one small bridge. The house occupied a commanding position just South of the Linge Canal and had been originally incorporated in our own defensive layout, only to be evacuated on the flooding of the island. It was suspected that the enemy might be using this building as a patrol base but this could not be confirmed in spite of numerous patrols to the area. It was obvious however, that it would be an essential pre-requisite to the enemy before they could mount their intended attack. It was therefore decided to send one platoon to re-occupy the "Castle" for 24 hours and so deny the use of it to the enemy as well as scuppering any of their patrols which might be using it.

An hour before dawn on the 3 January a platoon moved out of our outpost line and up towards the "Castle". The plan was that before approaching the building itself, two sections would form a firm base on the road and canal crossing NW of the "Castle". This was successfully carried out without any sign of enemy opposition. As soon as it became light the third section began clearing the outhouses and stables in the "Castle" grounds. This started without incident but the "Castle" then suddenly sprang to life and spandau and rifle fire opened up from behind the barricaded windows. The clearing section suffered 2 or 3 casualties at this stage and was pinned down in the outbuildings.

After a period of inconclusive fire fight, a party of enemy headed by an officer sallied out of the "Castle", but the officer was immediately killed and his men scattered.

A section of wasps (flamethrowing carriers) was then ordered forward with the object of setting the "Castle" on fire. This entailed these carriers driving up some 400 yards of open road, across the moat bridge, and to within 50 yards of the building all under fire from the "Castle" defenders.

The carriers drove up the road at about 100 yards interval. A stick grenade fell alongside the leading carrier without any material damage, and a bazooka landed a couple of yards in front as this carrier rattled over the bridge. The enemy kept up sustained fire at the carriers and by using AP ammunition succeeded in penetrating them in countless places. Nevertheless the carriers held to their course and successfully sprayed the building with flame. Unfortunately the building was too solid for the flame to set it ablaze. The carriers then withdrew covered by 6-pr A Tk gun which had been brought up 400 yards in the rear and fired AP and HE at the building in spite of the hail of spandau fire which was directed at its somewhat unorthodox and exposed position.

It now became apparent that the "Castle" was going to be a tougher nut to crack than had been at first expected. Consequently a tp of firefly tanks was put under command. Owing to difficult and icy road conditions it was 1500 hrs before these tanks could get into position and start firing at the "Castle". Although they fired some 120 HE and AP during the next hour and did considerable damage they did not succeed in firing it.

Meantime at about 1500 hours the platoon commander with his two sections at the bridge reported that 25—35 enemy were approaching his position from the North evidently with the object of relieving the "Castle" garrison. These enemy were engaged with Small Arms fire but continued to advance stubbornly. Artillery support was immediately called for and was brought down with great speed and accuracy. Controlled by reports from the Platoon Commander it was brought nearer as the enemy advanced and finally was falling only 50 yds in front of the forward sections. The fire was devastating, not only finally halting the enemy but forcing their few survivors to withdraw in disorder.

By this time the light was beginning to fail, the "Castle" building was still holding out and our platoon after a very arduous day and still isolated on the bridge, was running low in ammunition. It was decided therefore to order them to withdraw at dusk. So at 1715 hours they started to move back covered by the tanks. This operation was executed without further incident except for one tank becoming ditched on the way back.

During the night the "Castle" area was given a heavy pounding by artillery, 4.2" and 3" mortars. Some 1,500 shells and 1,200 mortar bombs being dropped in the area. This concentration was at its heaviest between 0530 hours and 0630 hours after which it lifted to enable a fighting patrol to get into the "Castle" grounds with the object of finding out whether the enemy were still in occupation and of recovering, if possible, the 5 men who were missing. The patrol was unsuccessful in locating either the enemy or our missing.

It was now decided that to assault the "Castle", considerable assistance in the form of AVREs would be necessary before the infantry would be able to storm the building. This assistance, however, could not be provided. It was therefore decided that a final effort would be made to burn down the building by using 4.2" mortar smoke in a sniping role controlled by an air OP. This proved successful and after an hour's shooting the "Castle" was seen to be afire at the back, and an hour later was a roaring blaze with the air rent by exploding ammunition.

This took place on the evening of the 5 January and was followed on the 6 January by the final action which consisted of a troop of fireflys moving into position to bombard the smouldering shell of the "Castle" and cover a section of carriers forward to a position astride the canal bridge. This went according to plan; the carriers got into position and a platoon then moved forward to clear the outbuildings and "Castle" remains. This was completely without incident and was successful in recovering the bodies of No. 1 and 2 on the Bren who had been covering the clearing section in the first action and who had apparently been shot in the back from a sniper in one of the outbuildings. After completing their task the platoon and tanks were withdrawn successfully.

Although this operation cost 1 wounded and 5 missing it was successful in denying the enemy a strongpoint which he could use as a base for any offensive action against our positions in the sector and also cost him a very considerable number of casualties which he could ill afford to spare from his meagre forces on this front.

Nevertheless, this setback did not deter the enemy from endeavouring to have another crack at the ZETTEN positions, for on the following night (6/7 January) one of our recce patrols making towards the "Castle" area, had not long left the outpost line before they contacted a body of enemy estimated at about a platoon moving South.

On the patrol's report, the enemy were effectively engaged with artillery and MMG. This provoked considerable spandau reaction which continued throughout the night. As dawn broke five enemy were seen approaching one of the outposts and were allowed to approach to within 100 yds before fire was opened. One of the enemy was wounded and captured and the remainder scattered into the neighbouring house from whence they had vanished when a clearing party arrived. This was the final move in the game of hide and seek in ZETTEN as far as the Bn was concerned as during the day it was relieved by another unit, having accounted for the satisfactory bag of 15 enemy killed, 7 captured and another 23 probably killed.

Such then was our life on the "Island"; constant patrolling, frequent minor clashes with the enemy. Add to this, the swirling of the floods (which later turned to the stillness of snow and ice), the roar of flying bombs passing overhead (with the odd one falling short), and the stench of rotting cattle drowned in the water, and you have a fair picture of this rather insalubrious existence.

www.ingramcontent.com/pod-product-compliance
Lightning Source LLC
Chambersburg PA
CBHW040258170426
43192CB00020B/2850